★ ★ ★ ★ ★ ★ ★ ★ ★ ★ ★ ★ ★ ★ ★

REPAIR MANUAL FOR UNCLE SAM AND AMERICA

★ ★ ★ ★ ★ ★ ★ ★ ★ ★ ★ ★ ★

VALENTINE L. KRUMPLIS

REPAIR MANUAL FOR UNCLE SAM AND AMERICA

VALENTINE L. KRUMPLIS

Order this book online at www.trafford.com
or email orders@trafford.com

Most Trafford titles are also available at major online book retailers.

Printed in the United States of America.

ISBN: 978-1-4669-2932-6 (sc)
ISBN: 978-1-4669-2931-9 (e)

Trafford rev. 04/16/2012

 www.trafford.com

North America & international
toll-free: 1 888 232 4444 (USA & Canada)
phone: 250 383 6864 ♦ fax: 812 355 4082

CONTENTS

★ ★ ★ ★ ★ ★ ★ ★ ★ ★ ★ ★ ★ ★

INTRODUCTION
★ ★ ★ ★ ★ ★ ★ ★ ★ ★ ★ ★ ★ ★ ★

AMERICA HAS BEEN on a downward spiral for more than several decades, our standard of living has declined in the areas of economics, education, morality, and world politics. Our image world wide has been tarnished by our political actions abroad [our needless lied in wars] and our trampling of our own constitution at home. We have become a debtor nation fixated on policing and threatening other nations and then attacking some of them for no logical reason. At home we have become a paranoid nation with persecution complexes creating government agencies like the homeland security agency costing us over a trillion dollars to protect us from so called terrorism that we fail to understand and analyze the causes off. The lack of understanding is happening because our politicians lie to us about the true causes of terrorism, our controlled mass media lies to us by telling us we are fighting for our freedom and the mass media claims that Muslims hate us because we have this freedom, yet we are also supposedly fighting in Iraq and Afghanistan to bring these Muslim people freedom. So lie upon lie is fed to us, our precious constitution is trampled by things like the Patriot act. Constantly we are fed a circus of stupid TV shows, we are flooded with non news like the Casey Anthony story, we are inundated in sports scores, all this is done to keep us from learning what is destroying our America, pushing us into bankruptcy and changing our way of life.

Imagine for a moment what is being done to distract us from important issues by the controlled mass media in presenting to us show after show about a mother possibly killing her child or not. For days and months this story is presented to us by the talking heads and round table discussions about this unimportant story. Then we are presented with sports figures and their use of steroids. Constantly these useless, stupid stories are fed to us, but information and education about important issues are not presented to us, such as honest facts about needless lied in wars, about our huge debts caused by the wars, about terrorism and its real causes are also not analyzed. We are kept in the dark about facts and events and even lied to about events that have real impacts on our lives.

As we are constantly lied to and kept ignorant and all signs point to a downward spiral in our standard of life, yet, we still continue to elect the same politicians year after year for decades and expect different results from the same incompetent politicians that have caused this downward spiral. This as we all know is insanity, doing the same thing over and over and expect a different result.

Today, Uncle Sam, has to roll up his sleeves, read the constitution, restore our personal freedoms, our rights to privacy, set up a diplomacy that is beneficial for America, balance the budget with priorities for our own people, establish term limits, and start fixing America. America must be fixed now because we can see that the elected politicians are now locked in stalemates, desperate, broke, and are trying to squeeze the middle class to support the crumbling big government agendas and the needless lied in wars they have orchestrated. Every tax, every fee, every license is now being increased to the vanishing middle class, these are the people that still have some dollars left. This is done to support their failed war agendas and the welfare programs for non working masses that politicians count on for their votes. The American taxpayer, America itself, has been pushed into a giant debt bubble caused by flawed welfare agendas and lied in needless wars. American people can be lied to, exploited and squeezed just so far. This repair manual for America is created to move America away from the failed socialist agendas, the perpetual lied in needless wars, the welfare state, and the big government of today. America today can be repaired by a population of informed, educated, voters using justice, honesty and our brains, all within our constitutional framework. This repair work today will prevent a predictable economic collapse that will result in anarchy, bloodshed, and a dictatorship that will come about to restore order. So to do things in a nice way before things get ugly, Uncle Sam should use this manual to fix America.

This repair manual is easy to follow. The separate chapters will first present the problem of what is broken and then offer a simple repair solution for Uncle Sam.

CHAPTER 1

★★★★★★★★★★★★★★

ILLEGAL IMIGRATION

ILLEGAL IMMIGRATION IS a problem that affects all Americans. There are millions of illegal people in America using our social services, hospitals, schools and milking the system that our tax dollars support. We all have to agree that this is completely insane, and unfair to the American people. So far we have seen our simple minded politicians present plans for a great wall on the border, more agents on the border, on and on with nothing working to prevent this flood that drains our wealth, brings in drugs, brings in gangs of criminals, and also possibly the so called terrorists. This illegal migration across our borders does not bring in doctors, scientists, educated people but only people who can not succeed in their own countries and so they become a burden on the American taxpayer.

When we have a national problem we should look at how other nations solve a similar problem. Is there any doubt in anyone's mind that nowhere in the world illegals would have the same license to steal peoples tax dollars? Go to Mexico and go to their hospital and tell them that you have no money, no insurance and no citizenship, and see what they tell you. Go to France do the same, go to the rich Arab countries and see if you get the right to steal their wealth by using their social services. Fixing this problem in America is not about how to do it, it is about the American people deciding to stop being stupid.

We are also paranoid about terrorists, so that today we have spent about a trillion tax dollars through a new government agency called, Homeland Security. They supposedly track the terrorists, and listen to their phone conversations, track their emails and so forth. They also spy on the American tax payer, they can investigate what we read, and when we travel by plane the American people have to display their privates and underwear. Yet, any terrorist with whatever he wants to bring here can cross our border anytime. How stupid does our government think we are when we are told that we can not secure our border. How insulted should we be when we see hundreds of people from Mexico run across our border with a few of our agents chasing some of them. What a joke on the American people.

All over the world nations have and had borders that could not be crossed. Ask any East Berlin citizen how impossible it was to leave the Soviet areas during the cold war. Yet we are told this illegal flood can not be stopped. Today our republican candidates for president for 2012 all swear to us that securing the border with Mexico is one of their primary goals. Their other important goal at this time is to attack Iran, figure that one out. Where were they for all the decades when we had millions of illegals run across our border and leach off our wealth. Why wait till now, when we have a huge problem of millions, to start their stupid blathers about securing the border.

Yes, Uncle Sam, you can build a border with high tech surveillance, heat sensors that will detect life forms and direct counter measures that will stop or disable any one crossing the border. We are today too humane to kill border crossers but when we get more broke and more miserable and our way of life destroyed, we will be more forceful. So please Uncle Sam tell our politicians not to lie to us anymore about the difficulty of securing our border.

By the way dear Uncle there is no problem with money for border security. All we have to do is stop spending 2 billion per week in Afghanistan and maybe pull some money out of the Iraq debacle. The lied in war in Iraq according to the Washington Post article dated September 5, 2010 will have cost us three trillion American tax dollars. Also the 1000 of our foreign bases all over the world are costing us 250 billion per year of our tax dollars. These foreign American bases protect all foreign country borders from everyone except we have not one American base protecting our own borders. Is it not strange that our controlled mass media and the propagandist talking heads never talk about the 1000 foreign bases and the yearly cost to the taxpayer of 250 billion. All this money spent on foreign bases and we are told that our parks and libraries and post offices will have close to cut the deficit. So dear Uncle Sam you must see that money is not a problem if we close some of the foreign bases. A good start would be to close the 268 bases in Germany. Germany is bailing out Greece and other financially strapped countries in the European Union so they must have enough money to protect their own borders from possibly Luxenburg. So please secure our damn border and tell the politicians that foreign country borders are not our problem.

SUMMARY OF DISCUSSION POINTS ON ILLEGAL IMMIGRATION

ONE.......... HIRING ILLEGAL WORKERS

Hiring illegal workers by any business, farmer or rancher should be punished by a fine and suspension of doing business. Hey Uncle Sam by doing this against any employer you are not loosing American jobs. Also if the suspended business has legal workers working and the business is suspended the legal people should get paid until the suspension is lifted. This would be a short process in repair work for America because employers are not stupid and would not hire any more illegal workers.

TWO............ RELIGIOUS AND OTHER SANCTUARIES TO HIDE ILLEGAL IMMIGRANTS

Religion is separate from politics Uncle Sam. Politics is separate from religion. Is this not what our constitution says? Any time a church or sect become political they should loose their non for profit status and should be taxed on everything they do and own. No church will want to bankrupt their congregation by becoming political. No church should go against government laws to protect illegal people. Can we believe that some sort of God wants to subvert the legitimate laws of America by asking churches to grant sanctuaries for illegal people.

THREE...... Mexico has a responsibility for their citizens

Medical costs, legal costs, transportation costs should be submitted to Mexico for payment. If Mexico refuses to pay then we should deduct that money from the foreign aid we give them to fight their drug wars.

If illegals end up in emergency rooms they should be treated but then should be immediately deported and their money confiscated and the costs of treating them and deporting them should be deducted from their money.

FOUR........

Illegals who commit crimes should be put in jail and any of their relatives who are illegal in this country should be rounded up and deported. This would force family pressure on would be criminals to consider their relatives. Is this hard to comprehend? Do the right thing Uncle Sam and prevent the ridiculous crime surges in the Mexican neighborhoods where innocent hard working people have to live in fear for their lives.

GENERAL SUMMARY ON IMMIGRATION

America was built on immigrants and immigration. Laws were made to allow immigration in a legal manner. Sick people were not allowed to come here, criminals were excluded and deported so why has the American politician today failed so miserably to do what is right? Allow immigration in a balanced manner. Close our border to illegal migrations. Also do not allow our government under the guise of refuge resettlement, like from Somalia, to sponsor mass immigration of savage tribesmen, with the help of naïve churches, and then force our rural communities, like in Minnesota, to cope with masses of stone age people in the community. The Somalis brought here believe in the sharia law, have no respect for women and are from a completely different culture. They will not assimilate but create problems in the melting pot.

Our national immunity from illogical immigration has been compromised by our ignorant politicians. The average American taxpayer has to learn to live with these problem immigrants while the politicians in office develop talents for earning a lot of money and move into gated communities where they do not have to cope with the problems they imported.

Going back to the fifties when I was an immigrant we had to prove we were good enough to come to America. We had to pee in jars for diabetes tests, they had to check our blood and our sanity so we would be good enough to come here health wise. Politically we had to prove we were not

Nazis, with no SS tattoos. After all this investigation, and our relatives putting up their homes as collateral guarantees that we would work and not become a burden on the American taxpayer, we the war refugees were allowed to come here. This was a good system that worked and we were forever grateful to this great country for the opportunity to come here. We also had to learn English and some facts about our government and constitution before we were naturalized. What went wrong from that time that now immigration has become a migration with no rules or controls. Simply put a country with no borders is not a country anymore. So we do have a problem, lets fix it, now.

The illegals that are here should be issued work visas. They can then come out of hiding and pay their fair share of taxes. The illegals should not be given free social services, free education, they should be able to have a work visa and earn a legal, taxable income so that they are not a burden on the American people. They must earn their way and work on learning English, understand the constitution and eventually get naturalized and become American citizens. A fair and balanced approach on immigration will be good for everyone. This insanity of thousands crossing our borders illegally while our politicians lie to the American people must be stopped. Uncle Sam has the money he can allocate for immigration repair by stopping the needless wars and fix this broken immigration situation. The American people want and demand this to be fixed. So dear Uncle Sam start fixing or we will fix it ourselves. In the near future if immigration is not fixed in a nice way and American way of life spirals down lower, and we become more broke and miserable we will form armed militias and protect our borders ourselves.

CHAPTER 2

★ ★ ★ ★ ★ ★ ★ ★ ★ ★ ★ ★ ★ ★

ENGLISH AS THE LANGUAGE FOR AMERICA

Hey Uncle Sam, what is wrong with having only English in all our government offices. Is it not absolutely stupid to go vote and see other language instructions on how to vote? When you listen to the politicians and hear the debates you form an opinion on how to vote. If you are so ignorant that you do not bother learning English while you live here and enjoy the bounty of this great nation you have no business voting. If you do not understand what the contenders are saying, how can you vote?

If you go for a drivers license and they have, like they do, instructions in many languages and your language like

Lithuanian is not included, you have to ask, why is this one not included?

Our road signs are in English, emergency repair signs are in English, so how can a driver who has to understand all the signs drive safely without knowing English? This pandering to foreign languages in our government institutions is stupid, dangerous and contributes in a negative way to assimilate all the people into the great American melting pot. We can see the problems in Europe dealing with diverse cultures. We do not want diverse cultures in America. We are all one people even though we all have different backgrounds, this is what makes us great.

If you want to maintain your own culture in your private life, please do so, but do not force the rest of us to pay for your cultural individuality. This is America, we are all different, yet we are all the same, Americans.

So dear Uncle Sam please pass a law that makes the English language the official one and tell the politicians not to pander for votes in different ethnic language groups.

CHAPTER 3

★ ★ ★ ★ ★ ★ ★ ★ ★ ★ ★ ★ ★

POLITICAL CORRECTNESS

DEAR UNCLE SAM this is one of the truly stupid phenomena appearing in the last few decades. Years back people enjoyed the aspect of freedom of speech in America. Today everyone must watch what he says so he would not offend anyone. You can not use the N word, which stands for nigger, yet black people constantly use that word on each other but white people can not use it even in discussions. Is this not insane? If you compare the evil quantity in nigger to the word honky or redneck or polack or DP how much more evil is the word nigger?

We have to remember that the two worst regimes in the last century, Nazi Germany and the Soviet Union were the most exemplary in political correctness. In Nazi Germany if you criticized the Nazi party or their war effort you went to a concentration camp and then probably went up in smoke. In the Soviet Union you ended up in the gulag or were shot. You also could have been lucky and only ended up in a nut house and were given drugs to cure you from political incorrectness. So we can see how this insane phenomena slices away at the freedom of speech. One word at a time, one idea or concept at a time is deemed inappropriate and we loose the freedom of speech. When people can not freely speak, criticize, discuss they become slaves.

We have a fine example of political correctness reaching levels of insanity in Canada. The Canadian politicians in 1977 created an abomination called the Canadian Human Rights Commission to insure political correctness by law. This ridiculous commission has a Legal Section in its bi-laws designated as 13.1. This truly stupid part states that it is discriminatory to communicate by phone or internet any material "that is likely to expose a person or persons to hatred or contempt." The opponents of this commission claim that a small number of people on the commission are determining what Canadians can and can not say. If this is not the most stupid law foisted on the Canadians then nothing else can be classified as stupid by human standards.

A Mr. Alan Borovoy, general council for the Canadian Civil Liberties Association states that when he and others created this abomination they "never imagined that they might ultimately be used against freedom of speech", and that censorship was not the role he had envisioned for the commission. Now this guy is really, really, stupid.

This really stupid man than gives an example of what can happen violating Section 13.1. His example is the book called Hitler's Willing Executioners, which alleges the complicity of German civilians in the Holocaust, and said that this book arguably "likely to expose" German people to contempt, hurt their feelings, and therefore be a violation of Section 13.1. Then we can argue that this historical book should be banned in Canada and the author put in jail if he comes to Canada. For this situation to be going on in a civilized country like Canada we must assume that there is something in their water that makes them nuts.

This political correctness is also found in some European countries. Germany, Austria, France, Lithuania forbid the display of items with the Nazi swastika. This attempt to hide history is so ridiculous that we have to question the sanity of politicians who pass these stupid laws. If we outlaw the Nazi Swastika from any displays then a movie like Shindler's List or Sophie's Choice would have to portray the Nazis without uniforms, maybe naked or dressed as Munchkins. You also can not deny or question the Holocaust. In Lithuania you can not wear a medal with the Soviet hammer and sickle. So this type of insanity is everywhere and is creeping into America under the guise of political correctness. Example of this stupidity is that on Ebay certain Nazi items are pulled off as not fit with their censorship but all Soviet items are allowed. Somebody should inform Ebay that more human beings were killed by the Soviets than by the Nazis.

Religious priests and preachers who use the bible as their guide, in Canada, could not proclaim what the Bible says about gay people without violating Section 13.1. Perhaps soon the Canadian Commission will ban the bibles and start burning them.

In America this political correctness has also crept in like a pile of slime. The works of Mark Twain are undergoing changes by removing the word nigger and changing it to slave. How can any sane individual accept this? These are historical facts. What will happen next in literary works when actual plots and ideas hurt some group of people, should we rewrite the books to make everyone happy.

So, dear Uncle Sam protect our freedom of speech and sweep out the political correctness advocates to the garbage dump where they belong and fight all creeping censorship that threatens in any way our right to say what we want.

CHAPTER 4

★ ★ ★ ★ ★ ★ ★ ★ ★ ★ ★ ★ ★ ★

HATE LAWS

THESE LAWS ARE the ugly creeping cousins of political correctness. It started in 1964, a Federal Civil Rights Law permits federal prosecution of anyone who "willingly injures, intimidates or interferes with another person, or attempts to do so, by force because of the other person's race, color, religion or national origin" because of the victim's attempt to engage in one of the six types of federally protected activities, such as attending school, patronizing a public place/facility, applying for employment, acting as juror in a state court or voting.

This seemingly innocent law grew over the years and expanded into an abomination. Today the hate laws increase the penalties for hate crimes committed on the basis of the actual or perceived race, color, religion, national origin, ethnicity, or gender of any person. Following this expanded law we now must be careful to leave room in court to argue how this victim was perceived or not perceived. Was this man carrying a prayer rug or was it a little carpet for his dog to sleep on. If I hit this man and it was a prayer rug then I am possibly guilty of a hate crime. If it was a rug for his dog but I perceived it as a prayer rug then I am guilty of a hate crime and get a more serious sentence. Now I can deny the rug perception and the court must now prove I thought it was a prayer rug. We can begin to see the stupidity of these laws.

Next included in this is the lumping in for protection homeless people and people with disabilities. How homeless must one be, maybe he just wants to live outside when it is warm, and for how long must he be homeless before he can be perceived as homeless. Next is the disability inclusion in this stupidity, if I hit a person in a wheel chair I get a more severe penalty then if I hit a very old frail woman. If without glasses I am almost blind and if I take them off before a fight, do I become a person with a disability and my assailant gets zapped with a bigger punishment. We can truly begin to see how government meddling to be politically correct can lead to legal stupidity.

We next see the sexual orientation individual claiming protection under this law if he just had one encounter with the same sex. How gay do you have to be to have the law apply to you?

Penalty-enhancement hate crime laws are justified and somewhat explained by Chief Justice Rehnquist's words," this conduct is thought to inflict greater individual and social harm . . . . bias motivated crimes are more likely to provoke retaliatory crimes, inflict distinct emotional harm on their victims, and incite community unrest."

The logical argument against the penalty-enhancement and federal prosecution laws is based on simple common sense because they offer preferred protection to certain individuals over others. This simple little statement trumps any argument for hate crime laws. We are all one people, Americans, and we deserve fair and equal treatment in courts.

In summary of this insanity I would like to leave the reader with a statement by Jill Tregor, executive director of Intergroup Clearing house speaking on black crime on white people. She claims that the white victims of these crimes were employing hate crime laws as a means to further penalize minorities. Her wording was, "an abuse of what the hate crime laws were intended to cover ". So we can see that somehow the white race should not have this protection according to this political correctness activist.

Dear Uncle Sam throw all this garbage in the dump and restore equal protection for all Americans and remove this smorgasbord banquet made for lawyers to untangle stupid conflicting laws. Have the lawyers seek honest employment, as hard as it would seem for them, rather then litigate hate laws and political correctness infractions.

CHAPTER 5

★ ★ ★ ★ ★ ★ ★ ★ ★ ★ ★ ★ ★ ★ ★

FOREIGN AID

Now HERE IS a part of our American structure that truly needs emergency repair. America gives out billions of dollars per year all over the world without any consideration of where there is the greatest need.

Dear Uncle Sam please fix this unfair distribution of our foreign aid. It seems that year after year the same stupid unfair distribution takes place. For example Israel and Egypt got one third of our foreign aid in 2010. These two countries got about 5 billion in aid from our tax dollars and most of that money was spent on armaments because neither country is a third world developing country.

Poor, poor Bangladesh with its floods and poverty received only 84 million for its suffering people. It is also interesting to note that in Israel our foreign aid in our tax dollars amounted per person to $ 336.25 in 2009. At the same time poor countries like the Sudan got $ 28.33 and the Congo got $ 5.07 per person. So countries struggling with civil wars, bad water and draughts, famines do not rate a lot of foreign aid. Today Somalia and Kenya are faced with famines. The UN estimates that 29,000 children under the age of five have already died in Somalia and that 640,000 Somali children are acutely mal-nourished and at risk of dying. Why is no one in congress trying to readjust our foreign aid budgets? The thousands of little skeletal children of Somalia do not compare favorably to our politicians to the needs of Israel and Egypt.

Uncle Sam please talk to our congress and tell them to adjust the foreign aid properly to save lives and make friends all over the world. We all know what the American taxpayers want in a case like this, so why not fix it? Why not demand our politicians to stop being whores who are bought by big money lobbies, and have them do what is right in helping people that need the most help. This unfair distribution of foreign aid will not fix itself Uncle Sam until we get the American people to become aware and have a free an objective mass media that would educate us in what is just and beneficial for America and the world.

Looking at another aspect of our foreign aid is that a lot of it if given as cash to the governments which are run by dictators, warlords, our puppets, and ruling families who steal our foreign aid tax money for their own personal use. How does a Mubarek of Egypt end up with billions of dollars in his personal bank accounts? So the solution for a part of our foreign aid debacle is to cut out dollar or credit aid and give product aid. When we give a developing country money, and let us say it is not stolen by the dictators, they may go out and buy a tractor made in Japan or medicine made in France. How stupid must our politicians be not to see this possibility. We are helping our competitors, Japan and France sell their products for our foreign aid tax dollars.

So Uncle Sam force the politicians to give our foreign aid money with coupons redeemable on American made products that are made here in this country by American workers who pay the taxes here to contribute to foreign aid. We can stop this BS if we demand our government to do what is right.

CHAPTER 6

★ ★ ★ ★ ★ ★ ★ ★ ★ ★ ★ ★ ★ ★

CRIME AND PRISONS

DEAR, DEAR, UNCLE Sam, what is wrong with you that you have not fixed this stupid mess that is wasting so much of our tax dollars, and manpower. All you had to do is look at some statistics on crime and prisons to see how screwed up our America is.

Anyway before I suggest repairs for this mess let us look at some numbers. In 2006 it was calculated that the United States had the highest incarceration rate in the world. In that year it was calculated that a record of 7 million people were behind bars, on probation, or on parole, of which 2.2 million were incarcerated.

It is interesting to note here that the People's Republic of China ranks second to America with only 1.5 million in the prison system. We also have to ask ourselves about the possibility that some of the people in the Chinese prisons are there because of political reasons. We know that China is a communist, totalitarian, dictatorship and would jail political dissenters. The most interesting fact about the numerical comparison with China is that America has one billion less people than China. Also in the world perspective America has 5% of the world's population and 25% of the world's incarcerated population. Yet with this statistic crime is still rampant.

Sooo . . . Uncle Sam, what is wrong with us? We have tried to solve this crime and prison problem for a very long time with no solutions or results. There are thousands of books written analyzing crime and criminals. There are thousands of pointy headed professors and self proclaimed intellectuals with symbolic letters after their names, PHD, MS, BA, and my favorite BS. There is a circus of talking heads pretending to have answers and appearing on our controlled mass media. Their spin about crime ranges from bad genes, race, availability of guns, on and on.

Crime is with us, has been with us for thousands of years and it is mostly related to economics. There are, and there were in every land in every time period, neighborhoods, ghettos, and areas where crime was the way of life for poor destitute people who could not make a life for themselves in an acceptable way. This crime phenomena had only one common characteristic, economics.

Give any kind of people a chance to live a normal productive life, with available opportunities to earn an honest living and crime will be reduced to near zero. However when we spend all of America's energy and tax revenues on stupid, needless, lied in wars we have no funds for our own destitute people. We have no money to educate them, teach them trades, help them become entrepreneurs, we condemn them to try to make a life in some criminal way.

As an example all we have to do is look at the black and Mexican ghettos to see crime running rampant. People are killed in the streets, homes, businesses. They are robbed, raped, mugged, and burglarized every day, yet our government does nothing about it. So our government permits the ghetto people to suffer. If this is not racism in the worst way than what is racism? Racism is not calling someone a name or asking someone for an ID, it is leaving these American citizens to live in neighborhoods that destroy people. The crime rates are so high there because there are no jobs and no opportunities. Simply put it is all about economics. If we agree that it is economics, then why not have our tax money bail these people out instead of wasting money on needless wars, and bailing out the greedy banks and brokerage houses who have fallen into financial traps not because of poverty but because of horrible greed. Let us not fall into the conservative trap of calling financial aid to ghettos as socialism, allocating tax money to help Americans by cutting out the waste of needless wars and foreign bases is an improvement in our budget allocations. We invest in America and our own people, is that not much better?

Before we go into analyzing some crime statistics let us for one moment imagine the waste of money in fighting the lied in wars in Iraq and Afghanistan. Three trillion dollars in Iraq and two billion per week in Afghanistan for ten years were wasted. Now imagine what could have been done with all this money in our ghettos. We could have created jobs, businesses, educated people and helped them extricate themselves from the misery of the ghetto life. We could have ended the ghettos as we know them. So why is everyone silent about this waste of money on stupid, needless, lied in wars? Why have not the ghetto churches, the preachers, and the people, organized and demanded an end to needless, lied in foreign wars and fight a war in the ghetto to free fellow Americans from crime, and allow these people a chance to participate in our American dream. Why do we allow these American people to live in a nightmare existence?

Let us now simply analyze some of our crime data. First we find that 57% of those incarcerated were sentenced for drug offenses. So over a million people are sitting in jail for drugs and we are paying about $40,000.00 per offender per year to keep them there. We can also ask ourselves if there is any logic in this when we allow people to drink alcohol, and smoke tobacco but not smoke dope or snort coke. We seem to want to protect people from doing bad things to their own bodies. Then we can also ask ourselves why do we allow people to eat and drink bad foods? Why do we allow food producers and fast food restaurants to advertise and push garbage and harmful foods on our people. So Uncle Sam if the government got out of the business of telling people how to treat their own bodies we would eliminate about a million incarcerated drug type prisoners and save $40,000.00 x 1,000,000 people=$40,000,000,000 billion tax dollars, per year. This figure of tax savings would also be probably more than doubled if we got rid of all the drug enforcement bureaucrats and agents chasing people on drug offenses.

We also are obsessed with our fixation on fighting the drug wars, our tax dollars are spent in fighting Mexican cartels, getting rid of poppy fields in Afghanistan, on and on we fight and the problem is not solved. Have we not learned anything from the prohibition of alcohol . . . it did not work. So Uncle Sam it seems that we can cut crime in more than half and save around a hundred billion dollars just by making drugs legal. The outcry of the goody-goodies and religious nut cases would be heard all over the country. You can tell them that alcohol has been legal for years and not a lot of people drink themselves to death. This would also be true for drugs. People would not run out and buy heroin because it was sold in the store. We would have enough money to educate people on the harmful affects of drugs. We do this on tobacco and fewer people suck on those poison sticks. The same would happen to the drug culture. Prices would drop to the floor and the profits for this business would be eliminated along with the crime of smuggling, and selling drugs, and of drug addicts forced into every type of crime to get drugs.

Now we only have to deal with only about a million incarcerated people who can be divided into violent crime and property crime. It is also interesting to note that in the years statistical data was collected from 1981 to 1999 that for instance in 1998 residential burglary rate in America was lower than in Scotland, England, Canada, Netherlands, and Australia. I am digressing here but it is interesting to note that all these countries have lower general crime rates than America but higher residential burglary rates. Could it be that these countries have disarmed their people with ridiculous gun confiscation laws and left them helpless prey to every scumbag burglar who is no longer afraid to break in and rob people. Of course this is the answer and Americans should be always vigilant against all attempts to disarm us. Violence and crime are not caused by gun owners, so leave these people the right to defend their property and themselves from predators.

Dear Uncle Sam now we are discussing over a million incarcerated so called real criminals that we have to support again with probably over 100 billion tax dollars. This is not fair to the working man that we should siphon off tax money from him to support predators that have attacked our community. We have to develop a philosophy that fits the time in our history that will deal with this problem.

If we go back in history we see many methods of dealing with crime that were successful. In some countries execution of thieves was a common and accepted way of dealing with them. America hung horse thieves and rustlers. Some countries chopped off hands of thieves so they could not steal again. Gengis Khan's son Chagatai ruled a vast area of land and it was said that a virgin with a pot of gold coins on her head could walk across the whole area without loosing a coin or her virginity. Chagatai was very cruel to the criminal element and so there was no crime to speak off.

Today we are to civilized and are limited by our constitution not to use cruel and unusual punishment, this simply means we can not kill criminals even if they have a hundred arrest records, we can not chop off hands of thieves, torture or mutilate people, so we have to find a better way to solve our crime problem. Today we are even pushed into an area of stupidity that capital punishment must be administrated in a humane way. This means if the state decides to execute someone for murder it must do so in a pleasant way so not to be cruel to the murderer. Is this not a stupid concept among rational people? I can not think of a real pleasant way to execute someone so his feelings would not be hurt. How can we make him happy as we kill him?

Dear Uncle Sam now that we have released half of the incarcerated felons for using or selling drugs we have to deal with the other half. The working tax payer must be protected from having his taxes support incarcerated people. Our tax money should be spent on the people that pay the taxes. How about spending money on medical research, education, lowering taxes, creating insurance nets to save people from catastrophic illnesses. There are a million things tax money can be spent on to make our lives better, our environment cleaner, than on using our taxes to provide a pleasant existence for felons. The felons have hurt society, they have robbed society so we owe them nothing. Is this a hard concept to understand? They owe us, we owe them nothing.

I tried a while back to propose a plan to save a lot of tax dollars on our prison budget. The plan was very simple, it was a win, win for all concerned. We would contact at that time an East European country and have prisons built there according to our specifications and because the expenses of maintaining a felon there would be about $5,000.00 versus $40,000.00 here, the taxpayer would save $35,000.00 per year, per felon.

These felons would be the ones that have a limited prison sentence imposed on them. They would be asked to volunteer to serve their sentence in another country and because of that would have their sentence reduced by some percentage. If you are serving eight years but you would be paroled in six we would release you in four if you serve it in another country. Think of the tax dollars saved that could be applied to so many good causes, or simply a reduction in your taxes.

Dear Uncle Sam this great money saving idea was rejected by President Father Bush and the stupid bureaucrats around him. I received a letter thanking me for my idea but they said it was unconstitutional to incarcerate felons in other countries. I did not pursue the stupid bureaucrats and try to explain to them that the whole process would be a volunteer felon transfer. Prisoners would opt for the program to reduce prison time. Maybe I should have done more for my country on this subject but I was frustrated by their stupidity.

My next proposal to save tax money would be another win, win for felons, taxpayers, and people needing organs. A felon serving ten years would be released in six years if he donates a kidney or some other organ to a sick tax payer. This would again be a volunteer trade, time off for an organ. A win, win for all concerned.

If we look at people serving life we should offer them some comforts in prison for their organ donations. They might be offered a big screen TV, or a computer, and a private room.

After all of our plans we still have a lot of felons and a huge drain on our budget. So Uncle Sam we have to make the incarcerated people become productive. We make them grow their own food, build their own prisons, make their own clothes and do a lot of productive labor for the government. It is unfair that the taxpayer has to support criminals.

This process of making people be productive would be a win, win for all concerned. Felons would learn trades, and professions, and become successful citizens when they get out. The money saved on the prison budget could be used to help the released people get better jobs and get on with their lives. A simple plan of having some of that money pay for some of the wages of a paroled person. Example would be a contractor would hire a house painter on parole and the government would pay half of the persons salary for a year or two.

So Uncle Sam instead of jailing our people for drugs, keeping them locked up like animals, and releasing them into a life of nothing, let us be creative and teach them skills to live, shorten their prison time, save budget dollars, and above all let us stop doing the same thing over and over again and expect different results. We must stop listening to the goody, goodies and all the politically correct nut cases, let us fix a huge festering sore of drugs and crime which have a huge drain on our budget and at the same time help our fellow Americans in prison or on drugs rebuild their lives and at the same time help pay for their incarceration. Everyone wins.

CHAPTER 7

★ ★ ★ ★ ★ ★ ★ ★ ★ ★ ★ ★ ★

EDUCATION

THE MOST IMPORTANT factor in the future of any nation is an educated population. Dear Uncle Sam and this great nation is falling down in the education department. Our children score about the lowest against other nations. We have to compete with the world and we do not do so well in the education area. Why is that when we spend more money per child than the rest of the world, yet, our kids score lower? We surely do not have a genetic or racial inferiority in brains, so what is it that our kids score lower?

There are many reasons for this and at the same time it is difficult to comprehend why a modern, high tech nation, a leader in the world would today have kids that score like some third world poor backward nation.

Something happened to our educational system about fifty years ago that led us to dumb down kids today. The main driving force in producing dumber kids is the perversion of our public education system. We force the public education on all the kids by eliminating choices. If a school in your neighborhood is bad, you have to go there unless you are rich and can go to a private school. Choice and competition is eliminated in selecting better schools. Uncle Sam, allow parents to take their kids to successful schools by transferring educational funds to whatever they select. This is competition, choice, which is the key to all our enterprises in America. The bad schools with the lazy, dumb teachers and incompetent principals will close down and the lazy morons will either become good teachers or go do something else. You can not force kids to go to bad performing schools run by stupid, lazy, incompetent people. How much more obviously can this problem of choice be presented?

Teacher unions are the most ridiculous entities ever foisted on humankind. A union created in the business world is at some point a necessary evil to save the workers from monopolistic, greedy capitalists. When workers produce products that make a profit for the business they have a right to share in the wealth. So business unions are good for a time, until like in our manufacturing businesses the high salaries demanded by unions forced American businesses to move to other countries. The workers all lost their jobs because no one sat down with management and unions to see the perfect storm in the business world coming because of globalization. Salaries and benefits should have been cut a long time ago to produce cheaper better cars and maybe Detroit would not be a ghost town today.

Teacher unions are a different type of union because the teachers get paid not by the product they manufacture, or the profitability of the product, but by the taxes that are put on the community to support education. The super high unfair real estate taxes support most of these salaries. This seems so unfair that an organized teachers union can keep demanding more money from the homeowner through real estate taxes. Why then should not the home owners form a union and demand lower real estate taxes? Why should the homeowner have no organized resistance to teacher union threats and escalating wages?

This mode of financing union teachers is further exacerbated by the fact that different communities have a different value of their real estate. The very rich communities can pay the highest salaries because of the high real estate taxes and the poor communities can not. So because of the way teachers are paid influences the type of teachers a community gets.

The bottom line in all this Uncle Sam is that using the real estate tax to pay for education is stupid and unfair to the kids, the teachers, and the homeowners. A level playing field must be set up where a child is not saddled with low paid stupid teachers and where the homeowner is not forced into bankruptcy by teacher union demands, and where choice and competition in selecting better schools is given to the parents. In summary each child is eligible for x amount of education money and the parent directs to what is the best school to send the child too.

This process would eliminate stupid, lazy teachers and incompetent administrators. The mode of payment and choice of schools would eliminate some of the biggest problems.

The problems that would remain to be fixed would be of the methodology and procedures to be implemented in school that dumb down kids.

The general idea that kids have all kinds of rights causes behaviors that are not conducive to a good education.

1. The idea that there is no dress code or general appearance code in school is a disaster. Someone must be extremely stupid not to see that a guy with a purple Mohawk will distract other kids in a class room. A girl with green hair and semi exposed breasts is a distraction. A guy wearing pants below his butt is ugly, stupid and distracting. Shirts and pants with signs and symbols also have no room in the school. How stupid is our society not to understand this. This is not about individual freedom, or expression, this is about education and about the fact that this hard working American taxpayer is paying for you to go to school. So if you take my tax money, shut up, and do the best you can to learn something. I am doing you a favor paying for you, and I want you to get educated and not dress or look like some freak that distracts other kids and keeps everyone dumb.

The repair for this problem Uncle Sam is easy. Make the rules and enforce them. When kids break the rule once or twice you bring in the parents and tell them if their baby is not dressed properly and their appearance is still distracting, then you explain that the next step is expulsion from this school and they have to go to a military type strict school where parents might have to pay extra, and rules will be enforced. You take rotten apples from a basket of apples why would you not remove distracting assholes from our most precious element, our kids. Why mainstream bullies, freaks, clowns, and rebels with kids that want to learn.

2. Discipline in class must be enforced in order to teach. Going to a catholic grammar school and high school we were subjected to corporal punishment and it did not traumatize us. There are other ways to punish but order must be maintained. Without obedience and order one retarded clown in class can steal minutes and hours from each student and waste our tax money, while the kids who want to learn are held back and dumb downed by this clown. Get rid of this clown. Send him to a special disciplinary school, and other kids will not want to go there. Parents should be held accountable for their kid's behavior and dress. They should be role models. However we all know how many kids have low life, stupid, drug abusing, kid abusing, criminal, lazy parents who do not care about what their kids do. How stupid do we have to be to think that these horrible parents will help us control, discipline, and educate kids. These type of parents will not do anything for the kids, who should be given a chance to learn how to live normal, productive lives. Special schools should be set up to save the kids from a filthy generational training they receive from horrible parents. Kids should be shown that there is a human way to live and they can push themselves out from the filth. When parents are bad role models kids should be helped by the community to become real humans.

So now Uncle Sam that we figured out how to give parents choices of schools and how to get rid of teachers unions. Unions that do not depend on the profitability of a product they produce but on the power of extortion they can exert over the real estate taxes of our houses. We can talk about simple negotiations of salary with the school board and community and some particular way on the federal, state, city tax system for funding education and get rid of the real estate tax method which creates an uneven playing field. Kids in Winetka, Il and Kennelworth, Il are rewarded and kids in poor Robbins, Il are shafted because of property value differences. We can now talk about education itself. Until problems of funding and discipline are solved, education can not excel.

Start out with testing the kid's IQ so we know what to expect from each child as we measure his achievement. Today IQ tests are criticized because they might hurt feelings of not so smart kids. Everyone is a winner, everyone is talented, no one is dumb, that is the mantra of the politically correct pinheads in our educational system. This is not true, all kids are different in their abilities and capabilities. The world has many opportunities for everyone. Different jobs require different skills. I took a test to be an architect in college and found out that my spatial perception was so bad that I would have struggled in horrible frustration to become an architect. It was great that I took this test and found out I would not be good at this career. Was this a bad and frustrating event to find out you are not fit for a certain job or career? Of coarse not, and every young person should be helped to find out his talents and his path to a productive life.

Results of education must be measured, each child is endowed with different talents and it is up to the teachers and counselors to guide the young in the right directions. No door should be shut to anyone in his pursuit of any career but truth must be told as to the abilities possessed by any young person and his chances of success in any field.

CHAPTER 8

★ ★ ★ ★ ★ ★ ★ ★ ★ ★ ★ ★ ★

HOMELESS

THIS IS A great concerto played very loud by all the bleeding hearts. They present us with numbers and misery indexes of the homeless. We are made to feel that it is our problem somehow. We are asked to contribute and help.

There are many different studies on the numbers of homeless and the duration a person stays homeless. Some are homeless for a day while there are some that are homeless for a year or more. The estimates by the National Law Center on Homelessness and Poverty estimates between 2.3 and 3.5 million people experience homelessness.

Yes, this is a problem of our own people living in misery, but it is not our personal responsibility to fix it. We must look at our own government and how it ignores a certain group of its citizens and allows them to suffer. Our government and the politicians we elect choose to spend three trillion dollars on the lied in war in Iraq and the rebuilding of Iraq, and two billion per week for ten years in Afghanistan, and maintain 1000 foreign bases, world wide, at the cost of 250 billion per year. This is our tax money spent on stupidity while our own American people sleep in the streets, in cardboard boxes, and cars. How is this insanity possible? How is this insanity tolerable? Time has come to fix this stupidity Uncle Sam. Stop all wars, bring the troops home and put them on our borders. Close most of the foreign bases and let Germany with 268 bases start defending themselves from our imaginary enemies.

Hey, the money saved from stupid wars, even 1% of it would suffice to build some camps for the homeless. The people, our own American people, would be fed, sheltered, educated and helped to get back on their feet. Our tax dollars, a small fraction of it could help rebuild American lives instead of our tax dollars wasted on lied in wars and rebuilding other countries.

Uncle Sam why not fix this waste of money and help our own people? Why not have a referendum by Americans on wasting money on fighting stupid wars or helping the homeless by using 1% of the wasted money. Is there a question how the American people would vote?

It is time to fix this stupidity. When the budget committees get together they seem to all talk about the cost of entitlements and how to screw the American people out of some benefits, but surprisingly nothing is mentioned about the war waste and the foreign bases. Our controlled mass media, presenting themselves as objective journalists, do not utter one peep about the war waste and the cost of foreign bases. Why is it so? By spending all the wasted war money here we could have created millions of jobs here and at the same time with a small fraction of the war waste we could have helped our own American homeless people. Why was this not done? Is it the incompetence, or stupidity of our elected politicians to misdirect our tax money so badly? Are they manipulated by the lobbies and other invisible puppet masters to act against the benefit of the American people? Why is our mass media so silent on this misdirection of our tax dollars?

Uncle Sam please fix this waste, this misdirection of our tax dollars right now before we get real angry and do something ugly.

CHAPTER 9

★ ★ ★ ★ ★ ★ ★ ★ ★ ★ ★ ★ ★

WELFARE

Whole books have been written on the welfare subject. Study after study has been done on the reasons people are on welfare. Nothing has ever significantly reduced the numbers on the welfare rolls. There are more and more people on welfare and on food stamps and all kinds of other aid. The costs keep going up, the numbers on welfare keep going up, and our politicians do nothing to get people off of welfare. A sane person would say that this is a problem in any society, but nothing much is said about this welfare cancer in our society and how to start fixing it.

There is no reason for anyone to be on welfare for their whole life. There is no reason for three or four generation of baby making families to remain on welfare, this is insanity. Welfare should be a temporary help and that is all. It should not be a means for a person to sit at home, watch TV, play computer games, sleep, while the rest of the taxpayers go work and support this person, this slug.

A common sense approach to welfare should be used to fix this drain of tax money. We provide the money for the welfare person and we should be able to direct almost all his activities if he takes our money to exist.

Drug screening should be mandatory for all welfare recipients. We demand that you stay drug free. The welfare recipient should be forced to work five days a week, eight hours a day doing community service work, if he wants the tax payer to support him. We work, you work, that is simple justice.

We will also not allow you to wallow in stupidity and ignorance. We will educate you and train you to improve yourself so you can eventually stop doing community service jobs and get a real job. We will also ask you to attend physical education classes where you will be forced to take care of your health. Since we are paying for your health care we should have a say in how you take care of your body. Is this not fair? If you do not like any of this then do not take our tax money.

We do not want you to stay at home and make more babies so you get more benefits. This is a fair demand if we are paying for your existence. So when you have your first baby, if out of wedlock, congratulations, but now tell us who the daddy is. Yes, daddy must understand he has a responsibility to support his baby. That is how the world functions. You make baby, you support baby. That is justice. What is not clear to anyone? Our politicians can not even understand this simple concept. The politicians keep giving more of our tax money to the baby producing machines without ever telling the daddies that they are responsible for their babies. Why should the working tax payer pay for someone's baby. Today the DNA tests will point out the daddy and the case is closed. The baby making daddy should be forced to work to support the baby he made and not dump the expense on innocent tax payers. So think of your responsibility before you make another baby. This rule would stop the baby making machines.

So Uncle Sam it is time to shut this insane waste of money on welfare. Let us create a pathway that gets people off this system and allows them to lead normal lives.

CHAPTER 10

★ ★ ★ ★ ★ ★ ★ ★ ★ ★ ★ ★ ★

HEALTH CARE

HEALTH, THE MOST important element to a living organism. This issue of health has been kicked around and lied about for decades. The drug companies have taken government money and research and developed drugs that they patent and then sell to the American people at huge profits for themselves. The same drug is sold cheaper in Canada but Americans are charged more. We can see volumes of paper reports about the cost of drugs, the profitability for drug companies, the unavailability of expensive drugs for many people, yet we have to understand that our capitalistic system is one of the best and the profit motive is what drives the economic engine. There is a very great problem when the system goes haywire, when the same drug is cheaper in

Canada and Mexico and we are told that the drug might not be well made in these countries.

Government grants for research should be factored in the cost of new drugs that are developed. The other factor that makes drugs expensive is the potential for lawsuits on some failed drugs. A drug company could be put out of business if enough lawsuits are filed. The costs for lawsuits and potential damages are one part that drives the cost of drugs up. Several things can be done to limit the exposure of drug companies to lawsuits. The first step would be to determine if the top executives knew that there were risks with a new drug, if that is the case then they should be liable and serve jail time. A supervisor who knows he can get years in prison will be very careful on what he approves. An unforeseen drug side affect can be blamed on the company but the legal exposure must have limits financially.

The same can be said for the doctor's liability. There have to be limits on financial amounts awarded by juries.

We have to understand that any award of millions of dollars against any drug company or doctor is an indirect award against all the people in America. Our costs go up with each lawsuit and award. Limits must be determined. If this is not done the sleazy type lawyers seek class action suits were the people get pennies and the sleazy lawyers get millions as they bankrupt whole corporations and put people out of work.

The insurance companies are partly responsible for our high cost of health care. President Obama tried to correct and implement great changes in health care and I believe failed. He tried to force people to have insurance. He should simply have set up a competitive insurance program that offered cheaper insurance and gave people a choice. To pay for this program and support county hospitals for poor people everyone should have been charged a small payroll charge and the rich should have paid an extra tax on their income tax. The benefit for all citizens would be that you would have a competitive insurance plan and you would not have sick people dying under your feet in the streets.

The president needed to fix our health care system incrementally not steamroll his agenda into the whole private system.

No one in his right mind would have minded if there was a fix on pre-existing conditions. A fix on care limits could have been done. A fix on moving your coverage from company to company could have been done.

No matter how we present the health care fix we are still to understand that there would be extra costs. Nothing can come from nothing so we are faced with more government spending. Government spending is looked at as creeping socialism, sneaky communism. That is right, it is that.

Why would Uncle Sam accept that? Spending some money on what is most important to American people, health care, even if it smacks of socialism is a great idea when you look at how America has spent itself into bankruptcy. Yes, we are broke because it is estimated the Iraq war has cost us three trillion dollars and Afganistan is costing us two billion per week. Is this expense on two wars not socialism. It is government spending. Our tax dollars spent on a war in Iraq we got lied into by a bunch of neo-con maggots. We attacked a country that had nothing to do with 9-11, had no weapons of mass destruction, we killed thousands of their people and lost thousands of our people. We prosecute no one for lying yet today after wasting three trillion on a stupid war we quibble about spending dollars on our health care. We call health care expense socialism, but what do we call three trillion wasted on Iraq, capitalsm?

Dear Uncle Sam please spend a some dollars on Americans for their drugs and health and stop nation building. Spend our tax dollars here, now. The benefits of spending money here will create jobs and make for a healthier America.

Few other things you should look at Uncle Sam that are really stupid. Our government subsidizes tobacco farmers to grow tobacco and at the same time has advertising campaigns telling people that smoking is bad. Our tax dollars spent on two opposite goals at the same time. Is this not total insanity? It Is Insanity, so please stop it, now. While we are on smoking let us address a simple problem of welfare people and prisoners in jail. We the taxpayers are supporting the two classes of people with our tax dollars so we should be able to dictate that they should stay healthy and not smoke. You want to smoke . . . then get a job and light up. Get out of jail and smoke all you want . . . do not smoke when I am supporting you. Same goes for drug use and alcohol. Want to drink and use drugs then do not take my money to support yourself, get a job.

Being free of drugs, alcohol and tobacco you will be healthier and save money in our health care system. We have to have it understood that when you take someone's tax dollars to live it is absolutely not your right. The giver tells you what to do, this is simple justice. So Uncle Sam, the giver can plan out a whole healthy life style for the welfare recipient. Yes, we can ask you to loose weight, eat properly, exercise and do a lot of healthy other things. If you do not like our directives then go get a job and stop taking my tax dollars.

Organ shortages can be eliminated by giving people a discount on insurance or hospital care if they become organ donors. Organ trade should be allowed with consenting adults. Why can not someone buy or sell an organ? Separation of church and state should eliminate this ethical problem.

Making this country a center for transplants, stem cell research, cloning would create thousands of jobs. The rest of the world is doing this and will grow this into a huge job source because of the changing demographics of rich nations becoming older and wanting to live a more healthy life.

CHAPTER 11

★ ★ ★ ★ ★ ★ ★ ★ ★ ★ ★ ★ ★

POST OFFICE

A REAL EMERGENCY problem surfaced at the end of 2011. It seems Uncle Sam that our Post Office today is facing a 14 billion deficit for the year. Everyone is talking about closing half of the processing stations, closing thousands of branches, laying off thousands of people, no deliveries on Saturdays. A great inconvenience on all Americans, small businesses will suffer, magazines, and advertising will be hurt, workers laid off, and all because of this measly 14 billion deficit for the whole year. Gee Uncle Sam, why not stop the stupid war in Afghanistan, it is costing 2 billion a week. Seven weeks, only a month and a half of no stupid war, and we have the 14 billion to save the post office and all the postal jobs. Let us do this Uncle Sam, stop the war for seven weeks and help America and the postal workers.

Or better yet after spending three trillion on a lied in stupid war in Iraq we should ask Iraq for a small donation of their oil revenue to save our postal system.

How stupid are we to throw our money all over the world and then shaft ourselves and our systems? Yes this is a question for you Uncle Sam. Why did you let us go broke fighting stupid wars? Why was our own mass media silent about this waste of our tax dollars?

It is not right that we will loose post office jobs and services for the whole nation so that someone in Iraq can vote or females can go to school in Afghanistan. Let us reverse the question, Uncle Sam, and ask an Iraq or Afghan national if he would care to donate any of his money to save our post office. After going broke fighting wars in these two countries we can be sure that there is no one there who would care if we had no post office in America. These people would not care if we voted or if American women could go to school here. So what is wrong with us that we stick our noses in all over the world? Is this government not of the people, by the people, for the people, American people is what everything should be about. The politicians should realize how we feel and do something to fix problems before we get mad.

CHAPTER 12

★ ★ ★ ★ ★ ★ ★ ★ ★ ★ ★ ★ ★ ★

JOBS

OUR VERY IGNORANT politicians all chant together about creating jobs as their main goal. Yes, good job, or any job shortage is one of the biggest problems in America. Lack of good jobs has destroyed our middle class, robbed our young people of opportunities to have a good life. The politicians standing in the perfect storm of job losses have nothing to offer as a solution except to cut taxes on the rich. This tax cut is supposed to somehow create jobs. This is total nonsense. The so called rich people are most likely older people that are retired or planning to retire and for us to think that if their taxes are reduced they will run out and start businesses. Even if they did want to start a business what can they manufacture here cheaper than in China? Would they start businesses in China or Mexico? How many jobs would that create here? We must also understand that the rich people are among us here, today and have a lot of wealth but simply are not jumping to create jobs here.

Our government, Uncle Sam, must begin to understand how globalization, a brand new concept in economics works. Globalization is still not included in the economic formulas today in America. The politicians and economists still use pre-globalization formulas to address our problems today. In the past the countries that made certain products most efficiently were rewarded with good export numbers. These manufacturers then made money and reciprocated by buying products made by countries who bought their efficiently produced goods. Hello politicians, this is not happening.

Globalization has turned these concepts upside down. Slave labor wages in China produce goods for America at fractions of our labor rates. Chinese manipulations of their currency also keep their product prices low. Our factories close and move to China or to some other low wage country. Our people loose their manufacturing jobs and go on welfare. Our country now has millions more on welfare while our dumb politicians advocate free trade. In 2010 our trade deficit with China was 252 billion dollars. China with over a billion people should be forced by our commerce department, our government, or tariffs to buy enough American goods to get rid of the trade deficit. China should not be buying any product from any other country that America can also produce until the trade deficit is reduced. This should be implemented with the application of tariffs if the trade imbalance is not reduced.

We do not know how to act globally on the economic level. Recently in December of 2011 we bid on an oil deal in Afghanistan and lost the oil deal to China. How is this possible? We are fighting and dying for a democratic Afghanistan, we are doing this for ten years and it is costing us two billion dollars per week and we do not get the oil deal, China gets it. Are we completely stupid and insane? Our controlled mass media buries this story [hides this from us] and most Americans do not know this oil bidding travesty occurred. It is not difficult to perfectly understand why this story was not made more public. Is this how we get paid back by Afghanistan, the American public would ask? So the nation building, neo-con, warmonger, maggots, who have control of our mass media were afraid that the American people would get mad and demand an immediate pullout from Afghanistan and an end to all their stupid, needless, lied in wars that have bankrupted us. That is why this oil deal story was hidden from the American public.

Another fine example of globalization type ignorance by America is the rescue of Kuwait. Here in Kuwait we have the princes sitting on golden thrones, driving platinum covered limousines, living in palaces, supporting huge harems in this super affluent land and our government decides to use American tax dollars to save the princes. Our own people are unemployed and getting poorer every day yet our government is not concerned about us. Kuwait is under attack and so we act as mercenaries to restore to the princes their kingdom to them, we sacrifice our lives and wealth and get nothing from them except bases to continue more stupid needless wars. Hey Kuwait, how about selling us your oil for half price because we put your butts back on your thrones.

We also sail the oceans and police all the waterways and protect all nations from pirates and so called rogue nations. We get paid nothing from protecting all the shipping for all our competitors. How stupid are we to spend our wealth to help competition ship their products We should charge the shippers for our protection. All this our government does for everyone but the American worker and taxpayer. Why is that?

Money that we wasted on the needless wars, money that we borrowed and became a debtor nation was not spent on our own people. These wasted trillions of dollars could have created millions of jobs and restored America to greatness. We are left with very little and now are told to tighten our belts to pay the debt. Our parks are closed, library hours are cut, our roads and bridges are in disrepair. We are asked to work more years. Our Medicare and Social Security is now something to chip away to reduce the deficit, yes, all this on the working man, the tax payer. The rich must not have their taxes increased because they create jobs. Well, their taxes have not been increased and yet jobs have not been created in the past.

We also have, not the brightest candidates, proposing a flat tax. Here we have the dumbest idea presented as a solution. The famous 9% Cane flat tax idea will be applied to a person earning twenty thousand dollars per year and the 9% also applied to a person earning $400,000. If you subtract $1800 from the $20,000 salary you have really destroyed the person's buying power and had a huge affect on his budget. If you apply the 9% to 400,000 and subtract $36,000 you leave this person $364,000 to play with and have not affected him at all. Maybe this rich person might buy a slightly smaller diamond ring, and feel slightly bad. The rich guy will never feel as bad as the poor guy who can not afford to keep his junk car running or to heat his cheap apartment or buy some medication. So, Uncle Sam, how hard can it be to see this flat tax as completely unfair.

Our government has started to address the job problem in the last few years because we have reached some very high unemployment numbers. The question we have to ask them is where have they been for the last several decades as our manufacturing jobs went to other countries.

So some of the concerned politicians voted for stimulus money while others argued against it. It was to late to cure the job situation the stimulus money just prevented starvation and people living in their cars and cardboard boxes.

So to calm the public the politicians told us that service jobs are growing. A lot of them in health care probably from Americans having heart attacks finding out that their country is bankrupt and their standard of living is spiraling down. Growth of service jobs is not the great solution because we ignore the fact that giving each other haircuts, or changing diapers for old people, does not create any wealth for America. It only depletes the money the public has by taxing these service salaries and then spending the tax dollars on welfare or stupid wars.

Example of this secret robbery by service jobs of the middle class to fund government programs and needless wars can be seen by the example of setting up a haircutting business among a circle of one hundred and one people. Each one of the one hundred and one cuts hair of the other hundred people and each earns one hundred dollars from this service job. Now they all pay an income tax of let us say twenty dollars. The government takes for their programs and wars two thousand dollars from this group of one hundred and one. We can see that service jobs create no wealth for the country and only tax existing money from tax payers when they do a transaction with other tax payers.

Our politicians and economists are too stupid to realize that the free market system that we worship has been compromised by governments in other countries where they help businesses gain market shares. Globalization has presented us with new rules in the economy. Global rules are that governments today interact with corporations to gain dominance for their countries. China today is buying up properties, mineral rights all over the world to pass this wealth on to their corporations so that they can dominate trade in the near future. If we think about this move by China and have one ounce of brains left we should ask ourselves what advantages have we gained by spending three trillion dollars on the Iraq war. Have we helped our corporations get rights to raw materials in the future? Have we created one job that is beneficial to building wealth in America with this huge expenditure? We have done nothing for ourselves. To top all this stupidity of wasted money, killed people, maimed people, the controlled mass media propaganda machine attacks candidate Ron Paul for being out of touch with reality because he is against the needless, lied in wars.

You do not have to be a genius to understand how foreign governments operate to help their businesses. A fine example was the good potato growing business in the Upper Peninsula of Michigan around Cooks, Mi. Potatoes where shipped to businesses in the U.S. Then Canada started importing cheaper potatoes that were government subsidized and offered cheaper prices to users. This caused the potato business to close in the Upper Peninsula. People lost their jobs and equipment was sold off. Would not a tariff on subsidized Canadian potatoes helped our growers in the US?

Another example in the same area was the importation of Canadian wood products which were government subsidized and hurt our jobs in the area.

Yet our politicians do not learn any of this and keep signing treaties such as Nafta, call it Shafta, destroying our manufacturing.

Our graphic arts industry was partially destroyed by allowing Mexico to do printing for us without any import tariffs. Our printing press operators were paid around twenty five dollars an hour in the nineties, while the Mexican operator worked for a few dollars. We can thank this concept of free trade in destroying our printing industry and thousands of good paying jobs. We now have cheap books from Mexico and China and thousands of people on welfare who have lost their chance for a good life. Is free trade worth the price?

Uncle Sam let us understand that Mexico and China producing these cheap books can not sell them anywhere else except in America. So let us put a high tariff on imported books that would pay for the welfare of the people whose jobs were destroyed by cheap Mexican and Chinese printed imports. This is the face of globalization, let us learn how to cope with it and survive. Free market theories should be left in the last century before globalization.

We do not understand globalization, we try to follow the old economic rules. These rules are that the lowest bidder gets the contract. Today China has bid and won projects, contracts, on our infrastructure rebuilding. They will rebuild some of our bridges, and tunnels. Some of these contracts are federal and some are state, county, city or some government agency. Our Air Force is contemplating giving a jet fighter contract to a Brazilian corporation after an American company spent millions in perfecting this jet plane and was producing some of them. So the American people are told to "Buy American" while our government goes out and buys from other countries using American peoples' tax dollars. With these low bid awards permitted by ignorant trade treaties we lose more American jobs. What is forgotten by our government in making these low bid awards to foreign countries is that they fail to factor in the cost of real dollars to America of supporting the jobless people, the closed factories and engineering companies that the awards to foreign countries cause. This is what globalization is doing to us. What chance do we have to get a contract to fix, and build in China? The slave labor wages in China, combined with their government subsidies and their currency manipulation makes it impossible to compete with them.

Uncle Sam if you need another example of doing business in globalization let us look at the debacle of Solyndra, a solar panel corporation. Our government gave loans of close to a half of billion dollars to make the business work and it went bankrupt. Again our ignorant politicians chanted a mantra of how president Obama mishandled the loan and on and on. No one in our government and mass media told the American public that our communist trading partner China subsidized their solar panel companies with thirty billion dollars and caused prices to fall by dumping their panels on the world market at low prices and thus causing Solyndra to bankrupt. This is globalization at work with foreign government subsidies for their businesses and we are blaming Obama. We completely do not understand how there is a need to have government help business in the global struggle. To us government assistance in the global struggle is a form of socialism. Socialism to us is perceived as being bad, but then why is it working so well for Chinese business.

We are missing the boat also on electric cars. The oil companies have a vested interest in making sure that we do not get rid of oil and switch to electric cars until they own all the patents and all the battery companies and all the electric recharging stations. So the oil companies, lobby, bribe, and interfere every way possible with a fast switch to electric cars. No one cares if the American public is bled dry by Arab oil as long as our oil companies make huge profits and place themselves in future potential profits. Electric cars will come as soon as the oil companies are ready to make a good profit by controlling that business.

Uncle Sam if you want to create jobs take the three trillion dollars wasted on the Iraq war and the two billion per week wasted in Afghanistan and build and subsidize electric cars. A transformation of that magnitude would create a complete transformation of our auto industry, we would get a huge share of the world car market and create enough high paying jobs to put America in the first place. The oil we would not need the Arabs can gargle with it.

Speaking of cars we should also ask ourselves why in Europe a car can run on gasoline and then switch to propane with a push of the button. Cars can also run on natural gas. In the Baltic states you can pull into a gas station and fill up with propane or gasoline, I have seen this done. Why is that possible there but not here? What makes this situation so ridiculous is that we are told America has huge quantities of natural gas that could power cars for years to come. Yet there is no rush to convert from Arab oil. Why? Why? We could create thousands of jobs by converting to this power source for cars, yet we keep throwing our dollars to the Arabs. We could export this power, develop cars with this system and export them, yet we do nothing. Why? Is this government run by the oil companies for their profit? Are our politicians that stupid not to see this?

Our bridges and overpasses are rusting and some have fallen down. It is not the London bridge that is falling down, it is our bridges falling down. We have to ask our ignorant politicians if the American people would feel better if our bridges were fixed or if we had good roads in Afghanistan and Afghan females were able to go to school. Spend the money here for the benefit of the taxpayers and also create jobs. Tell them that Uncle Sam.

All of our politicians talk about the importance of jobs and creating them. They offer only the simple mantra they chant, "cut taxes on the rich", this will create jobs and we will all be happy. What is forgotten amid these stupid chants are other means to create jobs. The SBA, Small Business Administration, is set up to finance growing businesses that lack capital, and credit. I have used SBA to grow my graphic arts business from zero to close to four million in yearly business. I also grew from two working owners to employing about forty people and all making good salaries. This was all due to SBA guaranteed loans and our own hard work. Computer technology and competition from Asian markets finally killed our graphic arts printing business but we earned a living for twenty six years and grew because of government help through SBA. We had created up to forty jobs because we had SBA help.

You really have to be super dumb not to realize what a great help SBA is to a start up business. The start up business has limited capital, no assets, no track record, and so neither the private banks, nor the rich people with tax savings, want to talk to the start up about loaning money.

So if our government is so intent on creating jobs why not capitalize on something that has worked, like SBA. The budget for SBA in 2012 calls for $985 million. SBA got $1.8 billion in 2010 because of the supplemental allocations. Today SBA is also forced to trim their staff to cut the deficit. Cutting the staff also means that requested loan guarantees will take a longer time to analyze.

So we can all agree that SBA is a government agency and therefore a socialist entity. Yet this socialist entity was and is able to help businesses grow and create jobs. How in the hell is it possible that a socialist entity can create jobs? Maybe a little help from the government to small start up businesses in the midst of giant corporations, greedy selfish banks, and globalization dominating the arena, is not a bad idea.

So, Uncle Sam, to fully understand the cruel insanity our government has perpetrated on us, is to compare the budget of a job creating agency, SBA, of $985 million for 2012, and the stupid expenditures in Afghanistan of

$2,000,000,000 per week. We only should ask ourselves how can our government speak of creating jobs yet perpetrate such a travesty in allocating our tax dollars. What kind of government can shaft its people in such a way and continue the BS in telling us how they all are for creating jobs. The other serious question on this issue is how stupid can we be to allow this insanity? Why are we not in the streets protesting? Uncle Sam convince everyone to at least show up at the ballot box and sweep out the maggots in Washington that care nothing about the American people.

While we are on the subject of jobs and socialist government programs that have helped to create jobs we should mention the CETA program under president Carter. CETA was the Comprehensive Employment and Training Act, it peaked at 725,000 jobs in 1978 in the public service jobs area. CETA by itself trimmed nearly 1 percent of the unemployment rate before adding in the economy extra money that was spent in purchasing power from earned paychecks.

So, Uncle Sam, let us do a simple pro forma budget based on the CETA idea. We employ 725,000 workers in the public sector at $10 per hour or $400 per week for one year at the cost of about 15 billion for the year. Now this would reduce our unemployed pool by 725,000 people and give them purchasing power to help drive our economy. All we have to do to get this done for American people is stop fighting in the stupid, needless war in Afghanistan for less than eight weeks. We are spending two billion per week in Afghanistan so why not take a brake for several weeks and create 725,000 jobs. How hard is it for the pinheads in

Washington to figure this out? How dumb is America not to demand that this be done?

I participated in the CETA program, in the private sector, in the seventies by hiring young people for half of the hourly wages and the government paid for the other half of the going wages. This allowed small businesses to get more help, grow without straining their limited cash flow. It provided young people with jobs and allowed them to get training and experience. This was socialism but it worked and helped small businesses and individuals.

The CETA program did not last long because the unions did not want anyone to do real work in this program and the conservative voters did not want make-work type jobs. No one analyzed the simple truth that jobs were created in the private sector and training took place. The good elements of this program were ignored and it was shut down.

Uncle Sam let me bother you with another pro forma scenario. If the government paid half of the wages for new hires that is, $5 per hour, then 1,450,000 people could be hired as in the first pro forma for 15 billion dollars. Employers could enjoy, and benefit with the extra help and be able to give young people experience, who in turn would have money to spend. All this can be done to help America by simply interrupting the war in Afghanistan for less than eight weeks. Why not do this?

Also an added benefit of employing 1,450,000 young people would cut down on the crime rate among the young. People earning a paycheck, having money, will to a big degree keep them from entering a life of crime. What is the cost to the taxpayer when we lose young people to a life of crime.

So Uncle Sam when you weigh the benefits of creating jobs, cutting the rates of crime, benefits to Americans in all areas how does that compare to the benefits of nation building in Afghanistan and Iraq at the cost of three trillion dollars in Iraq and the ten year war in Afghanistan at two billion per week. Is there a measurement for such stupidity?

CHAPTER 13

★ ★ ★ ★ ★ ★ ★ ★ ★ ★ ★ ★ ★ ★

GUN OWNERSHIP

Uncle Sam you must make the American people understand why our government wants to take away our guns, register them, limit the purchase of them. The motives of our government against guns are easy to understand, when a government abuses the people, robs them of their benefits, lies to them, wastes their money on stupid wars, that government fears a backlash from the American people. When our politicians take money from lobbies, steal, lie and vote to bail out their rich banker friends they do not want you to have guns. How hard is that to understand? How hard is it to dislike a government that allocates not even two billion per year to research cancer, that kills thousands of Americans, yet it spends two billion per week in a stupid war in Afghanistan. Americans are asked to run marathons, have bake sales to get funds to help cure cancer, nickels and dimes collected by the people who pay the taxes while two billion dollars of our taxes are spent every week in Afghanistan. How unfair and unjust can a government be to its own people? Off course, that government, understanding this travesty of wasted money, and that government rightfully fears an armed population.

When proof after proof is presented that confiscation of guns increases crime the politicians do not care for any statistics. When they are told that Hitler and Stalin were the biggest gun control advocates they do not care. When our prisons are so overcrowded and criminals are arrested dozens of times and always released to hurt, rape, murder innocent people, the politicians believe we should still be disarmed.

Our government and gun control nut cases have tried and are trying every way to make gun ownership more difficult. We have to assume that these gun control freaks either are so misinformed and lied to by our controlled mass media or are working paid agents for the government and fear an armed populace or possibly they simply are stupid.

Our founding fathers saw the simple fact that an armed population can resist tyranny and live free. Uncle Sam please teach all Americans what the price of freedom is and help America stay free.

CHAPTER 14

★ ★ ★ ★ ★ ★ ★ ★ ★ ★ ★ ★ ★

THE SUPREME COURT

Here we have nine judges appointed and approved by our government to interpret our constitution and rule on all of our laws. This sounds like a great idea to keep us acting within the constitution. However this sometimes does not occur when either the democrats or republicans control most of the congress and the White House. Each side tries to select judges that believe in their agendas. Liberals push for liberal judges and conservatives do the same. So the name of this game is who can appoint more judges that believe in their ideas of governing. This is truly frightening to the independent voter or to the party that fails to appoint enough judges.

Imagine a very conservative court ruling to reinstate prayer in schools. Making it mandatory for Mormons, Jews,

Muslims, Atheists to pray to the Virgin Mary and Christ. We can also see them banning abortion and condemning people to do the coat hanger methods at home. So the risk of stupid politically motivated decisions by the judges should allow us a better way of selecting judges or of over ruling their decisions.

First and foremost in our present system we should not nominate any judge that has a predisposition to some agenda. Any judge with any political agenda should be disqualified. Any judge with past decisions lopsided in a particular direction should also be disqualified. All this can be done except when one party has majorities and pushes for their agendas and appoints their puppet judge.

So we the people, our lives, our incomes, our welfare, our culture is ultimately decided by the game players in our government who manipulate the selection of nine judges who are appointed for life. We should be given a better opportunity to participate in the direction our lives take. All Supreme Court decisions that affect states rights, and group rights of people should be subject to a referendum by the people affected or by all the people. Example would be the abortion rights if ever reversed by an evangelical court should be put before the people in a referendum. An amendment process could then take place.

The supreme court judges should also be vulnerable for recall. Can anyone imagine a judge making lopsided decisions for years with no fear of getting fired. This is not a tolerable situation when we know that politicians play a game in appointing judges.

So Uncle Sam let us educate, and inform the voters about our flawed method of selecting and appointing judges.

An educated public will demand to have referendums on certain issues instead of having three hundred million Americans led by their noses by possibly nine puppet judges.

CHAPTER 15
★ ★ ★ ★ ★ ★ ★ ★ ★ ★ ★ ★ ★

SEPARATION OF CHURCH AND STATE

This separation of church and state is probably the best boon for mankind in history. All we have to do is look back at the insanity of religion mixed up with government and we will become physically very ill. Look at the Roman empire and see people fed to wild beasts and burned or crucified if they did not accept some imaginary fantasy God. Look at Europe when the Catholic inquisition burned and tortured Jews, Muslims, pagans, heretics and witches in order to save their souls and send them off to their God. Look at the Aztecs who in one day ripped out ten thousand hearts to please their fantasy Gods. We can see this today in the Muslim world where women are mistreated and punished. We can see the affect of religion today on the Arab world and their governments. We can only hope it will end at some time and a true separation of church and state takes place in the whole world.

So the bottom line is to keep religion and government separate. This seems like a correct path but it is not seen by the religious fanatics as a good thing. The religious fanatic even today sticks his beliefs and fantasies in our culture and our way of life. He legislates and campaigns against abortion, against stem cell research, against organ business, against contraceptives, for school prayer on and on. Some of his churches offer sanctuary for illegals.

The religious fanatics are always in our face with their attempts to shove their agendas on us. They even come to our doors preaching their fantasies and trying to convert us. Yet we do nothing to them. We do not tell them how to pray or when. We do not force them to have abortions or take drugs derived from stem cells, we leave them alone.

Maybe we should push for something against these pushy people to shut them up. How about us pushing for the complete separation of church and state. We can start by taxing religious people and religious properties. Why should the American worker support some tax free church or religious order. Make them all pay taxes and tell them they have the full support of the American people to worship as they please. That is the real separation of church and state and not what we have today that forces us to support different religions by not taxing them and putting the burden on us.

CHAPTER 16

★ ★ ★ ★ ★ ★ ★ ★ ★ ★ ★ ★ ★

BANKS AND WALL STREET

IT IS INTERESTING today to see our controlled mass media today describe the occupy Wall Street protesters as malcontents and misfits with no organized cohesive agenda of what they want. They are shown to us as fools who are there milling about with no idea why they are there. We have been told by some of the puppet talking heads that these people are too stupid to get jobs.

It is more interesting to note that when the Arabs did the some kinds of protests our controlled mass media proclaimed them as heroes and our government with NATO jumped in to help the protesters. We told Mubarek of Egypt to step down, we bombed Lybia to help the protesters yet our own protesters are declared as fools and arrested.

The Arabs protested their repressive governments, their thieving ruling class, [just like our super rich banks and Wall street speculators], their lack of freedoms, their controlled press, their lack of jobs, yet we fail to admit that our protesters have some similar complaints. The patriot act, homeland security, collections of misc. data, cameras on street corners, toll road payment data kept to show where we travel, airport scans of our genitals, gun registration, telephones mandated to have GPS, if all of this does not smell of "big brother is watching you" or of the coming totalitarian government to enslave and control you, than what does? All these intrusions into our privacy are explained by our government as a great benefit to us. This is for our protection and safety. Hitler and Stalin also claimed that everything was done for the benefit of the people.

So as the credit bubble might possibly collapse in Europe and in America caused by the greedy unregulated banks and brokerage houses our government struggles to prepare for a possible upheaval in our society. Gun registration, ammunition and gun purchase restrictions, internet laws passed to allow government to shut it down in a crisis, all these maneuvers preparing us for the day our financial systems collapse world wide because of the unregulated behavior of banks and financial speculators. The proof of the possible bank, and financial credit collapse fear that our government has is in one other simple fact of FEMA camps being built in many states. These are concentration points, camps, to house people. Today they are being built in many states with our tax money, again for our benefit.

First time I heard about them I was convinced that the people talking about them were insane. I believed our government would not do this. Yet when we search the internet we find out these concentration camps are being built all over America. After searching the internet I was so appalled to find out that concentration camps were being built with our tax money right under our noses. I called Senator Durbin's office to voice my indignation. The person that answered seemed surprised at my indignation and calmly explained to me that the concentration camps were simply FEMA camps being prepared for, again for my benefit, to help house me incase of some natural disaster in America. I should then be happy, grateful to our government for looking into the future to protect me from possible natural disasters. I tried to explain to the boob that Hitler and Stalin also built concentration camps but he told me to be happy and not worry. I am mostly concerned about the simple fact that our controlled mass media has not informed us to any degree about these concentration camps. If not for the internet we would never know what our intrusive government is creating for us.

So Uncle Sam please get the big government out of our lives, work on restoring our privacy and start to control, and regulate the greed obsessed bankers and Wall street speculators who are creating gigantic credit bubbles that when they bust they will collapse our whole financial system, and plunge the whole world into a giant depression and then bloody anarchy.

The republican party has been telling us that regulations in business stifle growth and eliminate jobs. Well we should tell the republicans that regulations of certain businesses stop them from polluting our lakes and rivers and air and keep us from dying from their pollutions. We have to thank regulations for our clean air and our food from being mixed with preservatives and dies. Yes, Uncle Sam you have to explain to the deregulation crowd of boobs that some regulation is good. Bernie Madoff should have been regulated instead of running wild and free to destroy thousands of lives and charities.

To further understand the need to regulate greedy financial entities Uncle Sam, you should teach the American people a new word, hypothecation. What this simply means is that a brokerage house or bank can use a client's collateral in their possession as their own collateral. There is a limit in America on how much can be hypothecated or re-hypothecated but because in merry old England there is no limit on hypothecation, re-hypothecation or hyper-hypothecation, or as banks would call it "churning" our greedy financial institutions established branch offices in London and re-hypothecated our collateral as many times as they wanted, all legal.

A fine example of this unregulated risk taking is that MF Global was able to "loose" $1.2 billion of its clients' money and acquire a sovereign debt position of $6.3 billion—a position more than five times the firm's book value, or net worth [Reuters News]. This shows us how our financial institutions through their greed and lack of regulations have exposed our whole financial system to a credit bubble that can pop any time in Europe or anywhere and wipe out our savings and destroy our way of life.

So Uncle Sam have the government stop tracking individual Americans, looking in their shoes and underwear when they fly and concentrate on the really big events like greedy financial thieves creating gigantic credit bubbles and then running to the hard working taxpayer to bail them out. Regulate these gluttonous, greedy financial pigs and tell them that through damn good regulations they will never get too big to fail.

CHAPTER 17

★ ★ ★ ★ ★ ★ ★ ★ ★ ★ ★ ★ ★

BUDGET CRISIS

As OUR STANDARD of living and our economy spiraled down and our deficits and debts shot up to trillions of dollars during the eight years of the trickle down economics of president Bush our politicians started waking up to this horrible debt and deficit scenario. Our media started educating us what a trillion was, a number with twelve zeros, 1,000,000,000,000. It is now explained as one thousand billions. The politicians now told us we have to work with them to fix the deficit. We will all have to sacrifice to fix this. Hey . . . how come no one asked us how the money was spent, the politicians determined the expenditures, voted on them and approved them.

Historically in the last decade our debt as part of our budget in 2003 was 6.4 trillion then when we invaded Iraq in

2003 our debt soared to 10 trillion by 2008, that was before the so called financial crisis. We invaded a country that was our friend and fought our designated enemy Iran. We helped them fight Iran by giving them intelligence reports and giving them weapons of mass destruction. They gassed the Kurds with our gas. Iraq was invaded because we got lied to about their supposed attempt to get nuclear weapons. The neo-cons and the talking heads in our controlled mass media lied about the facts to our politicians and to our pathetic president and we went to war against an innocent nation. Iraq had nothing to do with 9/11, nor were they a threat to America.

To understand how this stupid Iraq war affected our budget deficits and all these zeros were added to our debt we have to understand the weak mindedness of our politicians and our pathetic president Bush. This was the first time in our history that we cut taxes as we went to war and so we funded this war by borrowing. Imagine going to a stupid, lied in war, for no benefit to ourselves against an innocent nation and going into trillions of dollars into debt and wrecking our own economy and that of the world by causing the oil prices to go from 25 to 140 dollars per barrel. As we talk about budgets and what the two wars cost us and what Afghanistan is till costing us we forget the killed soldiers, the maimed soldiers and the killed Iraqi people. We have to look back in history were our pathetic president on May 1, 2003 stated that our mission was accomplished. This is the same guy who predicted that the Iraq war would only cost us about 50 billion.

Today our debt stands at about 14.3 trillion that we the taxpayers have to pay interest on. We owe China about

1.16 trillion. I try to remember that song about all the gold in California and from a hero to a zero, something like that. What happened to us Uncle Sam that we went from a rich, world loved and respected nation, to a meddling bully attacking innocent nations and going broke doing it. The answer in a nut shell is that we have a terrible foreign policy based on not what is beneficial for us. Our controlled mass media constantly tells us that the wars in Iraq and Afghanistan are for our freedom. They demonize the Muslims and tell us that the Muslims hate us because we love freedom. Today the drums of war by our media are beating against Syria and Iran. Yet, today we are so broke and tired of the stupid wars that we do not obey them instantly and hopefully never. We must all fervently hope that the talking heads and the propaganda machines in the mass media do not succeed in driving us into another lied in war and deeper debt.

To more fully understand the costs of the stupid, needless wars we have to look at oil prices in 2003 which were $25 per barrel and shot up to $140.00 per barrel in 2008. Today the cost is about $100.00 per barrel. The prices shot up because we disrupted the production of oil in that region. We can add the price increases in oil to our deficit because of the war in Iraq. We also hurt the European nations and other developing nations by forcing them to pay such an increase in energy costs. So we also hurt the world economy by our stupid needless wars. I can also see how happy we made the Russians and other oil producing countries by disrupting the oil production in Iraq.

It is also interesting to note that there were and are attempts to distract us from the real reasons we went to war. One of the more used ones is "we went to war for oil", this is so stupid when you consider we were paying $25 per barrel and ended up paying $140 per barrel. Today we are supposedly out of Iraq and the price is still $100 per barrel. So what happened with our supposed war for an oil deal, maybe it still is coming.

So Uncle Sam we can see where the zeros came from in our deficit. Now it is up to us to fix it. I am sure that you would recommend an immediate pull out from Afghanistan and give the two billion dollars per week that we spend there every week to each state of the Union to ease their state deficits. Every week two billion for a year and each state would have financial relief. This would help real Americans, our own people, to create jobs, have unemployment benefits, food, medical care, and many other benefits.

Why not do this right now, help our people?

Budgets are all about priorities. Our president Bush and his cohorts had no idea what were good priorities for American people. We were robbed by those politicians of what was rightfully ours. Instead of creating jobs, rebuilding our roads and bridges, helping manufacturing compete in the new global arena, seeking clean energy, electric cars, making education affordable, medical care affordable for all, medical research, our pinheads in the government decided that it was better to go to war and go broke in order to have the Iraqi people have free elections and give Afghanistan girls an opportunity to go to school and build better roads in Afghanistan. If this is not insanity then what is?

This insanity of wrong priorities by our politicians was not enough they had to cut ongoing projects in medical research. One of the saddest cuts was the study of autism of 100,000 kids from birth to age 21 at the total cost of 2.7 billion for the whole project. President Bush cut this ongoing study and chose to use the 2.7 billion to pay for a needless war and maybe build an extra road in Afghanistan. If this is not nuts, then what is nuts?

The magnitude of insanity, and injustice, in budget priorities is further clearly shown by the allocation of about 1.75 billion dollars, only, for cancer research for the whole year in America for the American people while we teach Afghan girls how to read and build roads in Afghanistan at the cost of 2 billion dollars per week. Is this insanity or not? Why do we tolerate this? The politicians tell us that the al-Qaeda and the Taliban are in Afghanistan and that is why we must go fight them there. I hope we do not attack Italy soon because the Mafia might possibly be there. Why not attack Mexico because they are hurting America more by producing drugs that hurt our people and cost us billions in combating drug problems. Thousands are killed in drug crimes, thousands die from imported Mexican drugs more than from our enemies the Taliban or the al-Qaeda.

Imagine the benefit of spending two billion dollars per week on medical research, here in America than fighting in Afghanistan. We would create jobs, cure diseases, it would benefit our own people and medical advances would create whole new industries with new cures and maybe address the new demographic problems of unhealthy aging people. We could be a benefit for the whole world, instead we use our wealth and also go into debt to fight in stupid needless lied in wars. Why is that? Every young person with a stake in this great country must research and find out who is to blame for our stupid, needless wars and our pathetic debtor's condition.

Speaking of priorities, that versus this, we should ask our government to shut down most of our foreign bases. Most Americans do not know that we have 1000 bases world wide at the cost of 250 billion tax dollars per year. We protect everybody from everybody. We have 268 bases in Germany protecting them from what, Outer Mongolia or Monaco or Albania? Uncle Sam tell the politicians if they have the urge to protect something to put the troops on the Mexican border. A real novel idea for our government priorities. Please enforce our federal laws on immigration.

Uncle Sam I would like to bring another budget expense that Pathetic Bush tried to implement and this was the missile defense shield in Europe to protect Poland and the Chech Republic from what Bush called rogue states. He believed that Iran or North Korea might attack them and it was our job to spend our tax dollars or barrow money to build a missile shield to protect them. This idiot idea was stopped when the world laughed so loud and President Obama recognized it as an absolutely insane idea and stopped this gigantic expenditure by Bush. How absolutely dumb and insane you have to be to believe that Iran might attack a country like Poland. So we saved some budget dollars, thank you President Obama.

So now Uncle Sam that we begin to see where the zeros come from in our deficit we might be able to fix it someday. America had a whole decade to accumulate this great war debt, over three trillion on the Iraq debacle, or nation building as the neo-cons like to call it, we see today, Iraq, a country fragmented and close to civil war. Recently the very brilliant governor Perry in a January debate proclaimed that we should immediately reinvade Iraq. He said it, but I think no one can be dumb enough to say it, so he probably did not say it, I must have dreamt it during the debate. Looking at Afghanistan after ten years of war, at the cost of two billion dollars per week, today we see no possibility of this wild land infested by warlike religious nut cases, ruled by our puppet government ever becoming a model democratic country living by the rule of law.

After this deficit debacle our politicians are now running to us and saying that it is time to cut the deficits. They tell us that now the entitlements, park services, student loans, veteran benefits, on and on they list our benefits that must be looked at and cut. They tell us that retirement age should be increased, benefits cut in healthcare, on and on. Yet only one intelligent man among the Republican contenders, Ron Paul, tells the American people the truth about the deficit in our budget. He clearly states what the stupid wars we got lied into cost us. He tells us to bring the troops home and close most of the foreign bases. But guess what, he is branded by our controlled mass media as a nut case out of touch with reality. He is insulted for understanding our deficit and speaking the truth to the American people. His poll numbers are ignored many times in the mass media. The media and the putrid talking propaganda heads have done everything to push this man into darkness and silence and brand him as a nut. Today, as he is recognized as a speaker of truth by the American people, and because of his popularity, the mass media can not attack his true statements about the cost of needless wars or his basic libertarian platform so they had to dig up some old newsletters to attack him with. Millions of Americans love this honest politician whose honesty is so rare among the pandering whore like politicians.

One honest politician like Ron Paul in a gang of lying, two faced, double talking, pandering, self serving politicians can not triumph. Here we are today hearing Gingrich comment on how things should be run, and yet he is the same jerk who was a consultant for Freddie and Fannie and got paid close to two million dollars. His statement on the fact that the Palestinian people were invented is so absurd and stupid that it boggles the mind that this nut has anybody voting for him. Yet I am sure this statement will get him a big donation. We can all see who the candidates are and we have to understand that nothing will be fixed in our budget unless the American people become educated, and informed. We must vote out the politicians that do not care about the American people out of Washington.

Further analysis of our budget shows us the pork barrel gravy train bringing us more zeros on the budget deficit. Here we have each congressman adding on special projects to bills in congress for his state or district. Here the biggest mouths, the biggest liars, the strongest lobbies, all compete for our budget dollars for their districts. They all want to come home to their constituents as heroes bringing money, jobs and projects.

This is all good for that particular district but possibly bad for the rest of America. What if a congressman pushes for budget dollars to build jets in a factory in his district? We might not even need the jets, they might not even be the right jets. Would it not be better to build faster trains, safer roads, have better schools, all this for more Americans all over our land. So specific pork barrel expenses add to our deficits and do not benefit all Americans.

In summary in order to fix the deficits, the American public has to become educated and informed so that the spewed garbage propaganda by our controlled mass media can be better analyzed and the lies understood. One of the first things to understand is that our great soldiers did not fight for our freedom. No one was going to invade us and enslave us. If we can begin to see the politicians and the talking heads for what they are we can start fixing problems. Getting involved, going to meetings, asking for answers, holding polls, surveys, referendums, and calling your political representatives and asking them to explain their votes will all contribute to repairing the deficit and the rest of the problems in America. If we act like sheep we will get what sheep get. We will get sheared and become lamb chops.

To repair the budget deficit we have to understand that slashing some budget items like wars and foreign bases is ok and will not create anarchy and revolution in America. To cut unemployment benefits, health care, food stamps will create anarchy and revolution in America. The Republican party does not grasp these differences in budget cuts. It seems that they have spent our tax dollars and borrowed money to do stupid things like needless wars and now want the American people to sacrifice their benefits to fix their deficits. This should not happen. President Obama fully understands the need to fix our budget deficit but he also understands that he can not cut benefits and bring on anarchy and revolution.

The answer about deficit repair is simple if you understand what caused it, and that it can not be fixed instantly. The hard core conservative republicans seem not to understand that immediate certain cuts will cause societal upheavals. They have no idea of what President Obama wants when he suggests more spending to help Americans survive the present recession/depression.

You have to have some understanding of what happens when you create or print money to pay for needed benefits today as President Obama wants to do. Several things happen, you help the American people to survive, you prevent anarchy and revolution, and you devaluate the dollar through inflation. For example we print one trillion dollars to pay for all the benefits and entitlements today. We now add that trillion dollars to let us say 100 trillion dollars that are floating all over the world. The existing dollar amount in the world is in computer numbers, statements, notes, bonds, on and on, and in physical notes. So the one trillion that President Obama wants to infuse into the total dollar volume in the world ads only one percent and depreciates the dollar by one percent. So the one percent devaluation of the dollar prevented mass rioting in the streets, the burning of cities, anarchy and death in America. The super conservative deficit fixers must learn this and understand that the one percent spent now and devaluating the dollar by one percent is the purchase price to prevent the country going into anarchy. How hard is that to understand about spending dollars now to buy time to fix the deficit slowly and incrementally.

Given some time, you Uncle Sam and the American people can follow the repair manual and fix the budget deficit and many other problems that are wrong in America.

CHAPTER 18

★ ★ ★ ★ ★ ★ ★ ★ ★ ★ ★ ★ ★

PEOPLE POWER

WE ALL WANT a better life with a good job. We want medical research to provide good health. We want good roads and bridges. We want fast and good government services. We want our tax money spent on us and our own country. We want clean air and water. We do not want to hear, press button two for Spanish, when we call a government agency. How hard is that to understand?

Yet, we do not get what we need and want Uncle Sam. What kind of government is it that totally ignores the needs of its own people, ignores its own broken economy, and is driven by some insane obsession to police the world and do nation building? What evil insanity permeates our controlled mass media which supports the policies of this insane warmongering diplomacy? We are subjected with lying war propaganda blather every day by the media and by the same crowd of talking heads that got us into the wars and this financial mess. We are constantly told that war is peace and security, just like in the book 1984 by George Orwell. This twisting of our language is called double speak in the Orwell book. Read this book which is a prediction of a society constantly at war, which is fought for peace according to the government. That government constantly lies to its people through the controlled mass media. The people are also spied upon in every way imaginable. Does this sound familiar today? We have bombed and killed people who have never attacked us. We are told the killing of innocent people is for our freedom. Is this not insanity? The Patriot Act, Homeland Security, airport searches of your orifices, your organs and genitals, library searches of what you read, sanctioned assassinations, illegal detentions, mandatory GPS in your phone, cameras in public places, if this is not George Orwell's book 1984 coming to life in our great America, then what is? How do the American people tolerate the same propaganda of lies, the constant demonizing of the so declared, rogue nations, and every day threatening these nations with sanctions and bombings.

What can we do today to get rid of the lies in our media and government? How can we change our idiotic diplomacy to work for peaceful solutions instead of needless, stupid wars? How can we get an objective, honest, news media? How can we demand the end of neo-con agendas in our diplomacy? When can we repair America's image in the world? When and how can we get our government to work for the benefit of America and all its people? How can we stop our political insanity?

The answers are all simple, Uncle Sam, we the people, must become informed through our own research, plus the internet, we must become educated, we must learn the true facts, we must challenge the lies in the controlled mass media and in the government, we must stop being dumb. We must become totally involved in rebuilding our great country. We must demand that our government work only for the American people. We will write, we will call, we will email until the truth wins out. We will never be silent again to allow the mass media and government lies to bankrupt our nation, start stupid wars and destroy our standard of living. We must do this right now because the puppet masters have recognized the power of the internet and are working hard to be able to shut down, and control the websites and bloggers that are speaking the truth about our bad policies

The beginning results of internet information and education in bringing us truth is in the appearance of "occupy Wall Street" protests, and the Tea Party movement. As we are becoming more informed, and educated we will become politically involved and work with Uncle Sam to get rid of the lies in our controlled mass media and get rid of some of the warmongering, incompetent politicians, and their policies that have caused this downward spiral in America. If we do this we will not have to organize an armed militia in the future, to restore our constitution.

We can also ask ourselves how can this have happened to a great and good country. How can this war spending insanity be foisted on the American people by such an uncaring government? This type of waste and insanity is done over and over in many areas by our government and the

American people are silent. Yes, they are silent because they have had a good life for a long time and have not became aware of the looming credit debacle and mismanagement by our government. The signs are around us now and people are waking up to the good job shortage, the foreclosures on homes, the increases in welfare rolls, the costs of education and health care costs, the loss of personal freedoms and privacy rights. This downward spiral of misery has been going on for several decades yet we did nothing about it. American people were ignorant in the self centered pre-occupation of their lives. We ignored all the signs of growing misery. Our mass media was no help. It lulled us into a sleepy state by not crusading for improvements but giving us only sports and stupid movies. The average American knew more about sports scores then the failing economy or the coming competition from world markets. The controlled mass media by a certain group of people had a concerted effort to keep us ignorant and teach us how to be politically correct while they shaped our government agendas, and our diplomacy for their own interests.

Our politicians were promising the same good things over and over without any explanation or knowledge how these good things can happen. Both political parties today promise the same things with no idea how to get them done. The people on the other hand have voted for the same incompetent boobs, term after term, as we spiral down.

We have to just look at the Republican debates to see the candidates spout nonsense after nonsense. There was Cane spouting his unworkable 9-9-9 and no one called him stupid. There was Rick Santorum the super good Catholic preaching to us about the precious life at conception and at the same time advocating the bombing of Iran and killing thousands of people. Then there was Gingrich proclaiming the non existence of the Palestinian people, yet no one called him an idiot or challenged this stupidest remark in all the debates. Poor Ron Paul speaking about the needless, lied in wars, and the costs that have bankrupted us, and the stupid plans to attack Iran was looked at by the others as being out of touch with the real truth. We can see from the debates that if one of these candidates, except for Ron Paul, gets elected we will have more stupid wars, no peace in the middle east, more debt and no prosecution of the neo-con liars that got us into the Iraq war. It is also interesting to note that after Ron Paul speaks out the neo-con talking heads are dragged out on the news to inform us of how horrible Ron Paul's platform for peace is, and that war and debt is better according to these maggots. Ron Paul is branded an isolationist because he does not believe in attacking nations that have not attacked us and have no capability of making war on us.

The question Uncle Sam is why would anyone vote for the same politicians over and over again while things are going worse and worse? Why not vote for new people, new political parties. We see our two parties locked in a stalemate today. They care only how to win against each other and not how to stop arguments and do something for the American people. Time surely has come today to get rid of all the old politicians and blaze a new way with the internet communications, with referendums, and opinion polls conducted outside of the controlled mass media. Let us get rid of the talking maggot heads with their agendas and their pandering to special interest lobbies. A real, binding referendum, by the American people, should demand a free objective mass media for America. The American people deserve a free objective media instead of a controlled propaganda tool by the lobbies. Free the press and people will be free.

Uncle Sam make the American people understand that the two political parties we have pander to specific groups of people where they get the votes and the money. The Democrats pander to the minorities, the unions, the welfare people, and not to the general public. The Republicans pander to the rich, the corporations, and the war profiteers, and the so called evangelicals. Both of these parties are bought and paid for by special interest lobbies. This leaves the hard working middle class with no one representing them to any high degree. We, the middle class workers, the silent majority, the tax payers have lost our government representatives. We do not have a lobby that represents us. We have no lobby that donates/bribes the politicians to vote for us. Today we have a fairly even number of different panderers opposing each other in congress and that is why we have the stalemates on most issues. They seem to only agree on only two issues and that is war and more war and higher debt. We have to ask ourselves why that is and why only poor Ron Paul preaches against the needless wars. We also have to ask ourselves why our controlled mass media constantly portrays Ron Paul as some kind of nut case because he is anti war. Why is that? Who profits from war spending? Who benefits from regime changes in the Middle East? For sure it is not the American people.

Uncle Sam by himself can not repair America. He must have the help of an educated, informed population. We must clear our minds of propaganda by the controlled mass media and the hired talking head prostitutes that perform for the benefit of certain lobby groups. We can clear our minds by going to the internet for some answers and also getting news from other countries. The availability of various news services on the internet, cable, satellites makes it almost impossible for our controlled mass media to keep us ignorant of the truth. It is our choice to learn the truth and help Uncle Sam fix America, the land we love. We must take back our constitution and establish a government that represents the American people. Our government should have a clearly defined duty to concentrate on our welfare and not run around the world nation building and acting as the policeman of the world. We must remember the old saying "who died and left you in charge", no one died and the world did not ask us to become world policemen. As some kind of insane world police force we are made to feel, by neo-con lies, justified in having thousands of our young people killed and maimed while we kill hundreds of thousands of our so called enemies. We do all this foreign insanity while our global competitors in the economic competition gain all the advantages against us while we sink into trillions of dollars of debt and loose our standard of living.

It is time for real change, real repair work, American people are a just people and crave the good life and all they have to do is get informed and become politically involved to help Uncle Sam repair America.

-NOTES-

-NOTES-

-NOTES-